A BOOK OF INSPIRATIONAL POETRY

CLIMB THE
Red
MOUNTAIN

Byron von Rosenberg

ACW Press
Eugene, Oregon 97405

Climb the Red Mountain
Copyright ©2004 Byron von Rosenberg
All rights reserved

Cover Design by Alpha Advertising
Interior design by Pine Hill Graphics

Packaged by ACW Press
85334 Lorane Hwy
Eugene, Oregon 97405
www.acwpress.com
The views expressed or implied in this work do not necessarily reflect those of ACW Press. Ultimate design, content, and editorial accuracy of this work is the responsibility of the author(s).

Publisher's Cataloging-in-Publication Data
(Provided by Cassidy Cataloguing Services, Inc.)

von Rosenberg, Byron.

   Climb the red mountain : a book of inspirational poetry / Byron von Rosenberg. -- 1st ed. -- Eugene, Ore. : ACW Press, 2004.

    p. ; cm.

   ISBN: 1-932124-23-3

   1. Inspiration--Poetry. 2. Poetry. 3. Religious poetry. I. Title.

PS3618.R674 A17 2004
811/.6--dc22   0401

Printed in the United States of America.

Dedication

---

*T*his book is dedicated to my wife, Sharon. I thank God that the person I love also loves me, and I'm glad for every new day that Sharon sails through life with me.

Sail with Me Tomorrow

Sail with me tomorrow
    And feel the mist and spray,
For the wind is strong behind us
    And the sun sparkles on the bay.
From the river's mouth we'll sail
    And set our course far out to sea.
The ebbing tide is pulling us
    So won't you sail with me?
The clouds on far horizons
    Mean naught to hardy souls
For our ship will never founder
    Or break upon the shoals.
There is no path to follow,
    Our destination not yet known,
And just the two of us will go,
    At last, we're on our own.
Ah, the joy and price of freedom,
    We must leave the place we know,
But we hear the ocean calling
    And we will surely go.
So sail with me tomorrow
    On a trip to forever's shores
For the greatest journey ever—
    This one!—mine and yours.

May God bless you on your journey through this book and on your journey through life.

Sincerely,

Byron von Rosenberg
House Springs, Missouri
September 6, 2003

Acknowledgments

I believe that God sometimes chooses to give people talents outside of their training so that they will joyfully and willingly give Him the honor, praise, and glory for that gift. In this way, others may come to understand that all things are truly possible with Him and that the promise of His kingdom is true. My undergraduate degree is in engineering and I work as a sales manager. Yet people enjoy the ideas, the stories, and, yes, even the rhymes I write. And so, should you find in these pages a poem that has special meaning for you, the glory belongs to God alone. And you may be sure He intended for you to find that message when He gave the poem to me to write.

I wish to thank my immediate family for their love and patience with me as I continue my writing. Sharon, Ryan, and Erin have each given up time with me so I can pursue this wonderful gift. I know they do not always understand, but they are always understanding. Thank you each so very, very much.

For everyone who has prayed for us, I am truly grateful. And I wish to thank everyone who supported our efforts by purchasing *Don't Feed the Seagulls*, my first book. Special thanks goes to Marjorie, Gene, Clyde, Charles, and Caroline von Rosenberg, to Carol Engle, and to their families. I offer my thanks to Joe Galbraith, to the Scouts and Scouters of Boy Scout Troop 387, and to the members of the St. Louis West Optimist Club. I have also been inspired by the residents of Sun City in Georgetown, Texas, especially the members of the Let's Talk About It Wednesday Afternoon Book Club that Meets on Friday Mornings, the Sun City Kiwanis Club and Georgetown Optimists. God bless you all!

I do considerable writing at Forest Park in St. Louis. It is a lovely place that provides beauty and inspiration. My special thanks go to the people who work so hard to keep it clean and to those who seek to preserve its beauty through the efforts of Forest Park Forever.

I also write at the Laumeier Sculpture Park. It is a place that encourages creativity through its combination of natural and man-made beauty and I thank those who work to preserve it.

There is a little park near my home in Byrnes Mill where I can sit, write, and watch the sunset. The park was recently donated to the city by two local citizens and I thank them for their generosity. The beauty of Jefferson County has inspired many poems.

Finally, I'd like to thank you, the reader. May you find that special poem and message sent just for you.

Sincerely,

Byron von Rosenberg
House Springs, Missouri
August 18, 2003

Contents

Foreword. 10

1. Climb the Red Mountain 13

    Climb the Red Mountain. 13
    When the Last Cloud's Past. 15
    While I Wait, I Run. 18
    Five. 18
    Sail the Rainbow. 19
    Shining through the Rain 20

2. Barefoot on Roses 21

    Barefoot on Roses. 21
    The Rose-Red Snow at Sunrise 22
    Yesterday's Snow Is Gone. 22
    Picnic by the River 23
    Dinner by Candlelight 23
    Dance in the Moonlight. 24
    Touched by a Rose Petal. 25
    Raindrops and Kisses 25
    I Love You in the Summer Rain 26
    A Simple Place for Love to Start 27
    Just One Star 27
    One Kiss for All the Roses 28

3. I'll Still Fly 29

    I'll Still Fly. 29
    If I Crash 30
    Vapor Trails. 30
    Our Outstretched Wings 31
    The Eagle Rises 32

4. Footsteps in the Garden 34

    Footsteps in the Garden. 34
    One Strong Heart. 36
    Come Away 37
    Always Watch Me 37
    A Different Race 38
    A Shelter in the Rock 40

The Forgotten Gift 41
Hope for a Heartbeat 42
The Three-Word Gospel 44

5. The Sound of Freedom's Sail 45
The Sound of Freedom's Sail 45
On the Fringe 46
Where Freedom Lives 47
With the Seasons 48
Just One Hundred 49
Three Scouts Left 50

6. Stained Glass Garden Window 51
Stained Glass Garden Window 51
Thomas Dowden 52
Irish Soda Bread 54
More Than Ever 54
Light Friendly Snows 55
Stone Pillars 56
Castles in the Sand 56
All That's Left 57
Grandma's Gardenias 58
Puddles by the Roses 58
Last of the Season Run 59

7. Walter Wupperman's Wings 61
Walter Wupperman's Wings 61
Thinking Upside Down 62
Leading the Unicorn 63
Hanging Stars and Planets 63
Lost and Found for Dreams 64
Russian Language Music 65
El Emeno 66
Glue 67
The Kettle, the Pot and What They Were Not 67
The Thread's View 68
Fielder's Choice 68
Life of the Party 69
Turnabout Mountain 70
High on Heaven's Rope 71

8. The Dead Snake's Bite 73
The Dead Snake's Bite 73
The Breath Holding Contest 74
The Little Pyromaniac 74

Sinbad and the Golden Horseshoes 75
Bigger Than a Cement Truck. 76

9. **The Seagull Looked** **78**

The Seagull Looked 78
Don't Scratch! 79
Ivan the Terrier 79
Amall the Llama 80
Opaki…I Mean, Okapi! 81
The Llama's Bunny Ears. 82
The Eagle's View 83

9. **I Don't Wanna Kiss a Llama** **84**

I Don't Wanna Kiss a Llama 84
King Louie's Horse's Butt: A Love Story. 85
The Two-Toed Sloth Learns to Count 86
Super-Frog Gets a Gig 87
Friday the Thirteenth 87
Oh Christmas Treed 88
Santa's New Suit 89
An Apology to Camels 90

Epilogue **93**

A Lone Connection 93

Don't Feed the Seagulls **96**

Note: A Seagull ( ) at the
end of a page indicates that
the same poem continues on
the next page.

Foreword

————

A's engineering students, we rode on the University of Tulsa bus to classes on the school's other campus that morning in 1977. Beside me was Byron, a chemical engineering student. As we got off the bus, our talk was veering from small talk to issues of life in Christ. In fact, we would soon be praying in a corner of the hall and affirming the lordship of Christ in our lives before heading off to our classes that day. A friendship started that later included Gene and Clyde, his brothers, and Dr. von Rosenberg, his father, who made my introductory engineering science class the most interesting I could have wished for.

Over the years I have observed Byron, the 'A' grade chemical engineering graduate, move from that field of endeavor to involvement with the Boy Scouts and now, at my last check, writing books of poetry. I have also had my twists and turns: I have lived and worked on three continents as a petroleum engineer, and I am now a visiting professor of business management in Asia.

There is a common string that runs through our lives, Byron and I: the freedom to follow our dreams no matter what changes come as a result. It is an adventure to live as a disciple of Jesus and dare to become something new as life moves on. Jesus said, "Follow me and I will make you…"

This new book speaks to the heart of the trailblazer, the mountain climber, the spirit of the overcomer. Find in these pages the beauty of love for family, mother, and sweetheart. Read also of love both for one's nation and the contemporary heroes of that nation. Grieve at the great loss of those frontier breakers on the space shuttle that disintegrated on its return flight to earth. Go with Byron from the very mundane subjects to the most sublime, and see through the eyes of a disciple how life fits when lived under Jesus' lordship.

As you read this book, dare to dream. Dare to let God fulfill your most sublime dreams. In his book *Daring to Live on the Edge*, Loren Cunningham writes of experiencing the God of the universe in each of our lives so that we are "spoilt for the ordinary." There's just one life to live down here; dare to let yours count for the Creator.

I recommend this book to every person—no matter what age you are—whose heart beats for adventure, for freedom from routines, for romance, for meaning in God that is lived out practically on planet Earth. Someone has rightly said, "Don't be so heavenly minded that you are no earthly use."

Thanks, Byron, for the great privilege to introduce this book, not only because it is a great book, but because I know the author whose worth has been tested and confirmed "great" over many years of real friendship.

Meshack Ilobi
Cooperative Studies Inc. USA
Visiting Professor
University of Dhaka
Bangladesh
September 11, 2003

———

Chapter One

Climb the Red Mountain

Climb the Red Mountain

Only for an instant,
    Late in the waning year,
Only one place to see it
    And I am standing here.
The leaves have turned from green
    To orange, yellow, and brown
And are red only on the mountain
    Just as the sun goes down.
Beautiful beyond belief,
    I am the only one who sees it.
This chance may come but once;
    I must act now to seize it!
Climb the crimson mountain slopes
    As the sun sinks low in the sky!
What will I find when I reach the top?
    I won't know unless I try!

I set out on the upward trail
    And come around the bend,
Impeded by a rocky cliff
    That dares me to ascend.
The one I was another time
    Would soon have turned away,

But faith has made me stronger
    And I'll not retreat today!
It hurts to grip the rock
    And my progress is so slow;
But suddenly I find a ledge—
    The trail!—and off I go.
Will I reach the top
    Before the setting of the sun?
I see the peak against the sky
    And break into a run.
What view of glory did I find
    Atop this crimson shelf?
For you to find the answer
    You must climb up here yourself.

Do not mistake my challenge
    And think I do not care,
But this decision's up to you
    And you alone must dare.
For if you're to reach the summit
    And touch the ruby sky,
It will take your everything—
    Your fierce, determined try!
The obstacles you encounter
    Will strengthen you within,
Though you may stumble near the top
    And have to start again.
But if you keep your focus
    And stray not from the trail,
You'll win the victory inside—
    It's then you cannot fail.
Ascend the fiery mountain!
    Be awed by God's grand view!
Persevere in noble goals,
    It's what you have to do.

It will test your faith
    As these steep slopes you climb
But when your spirit's empty
    God fills it every time!
Never doubt yourself
    Or what you can achieve.
All is possible with Him
    But first you must believe.
So when your body's weary
    And every muscle stings,
Lift your eyes up to the heavens
    And rise on eagles' wings!
For when you build your life
    As God would have it be
You will make it to the top
    And He will set you free.
So climb the crimson mountain slopes
    As the sun sinks low in the sky!
What will you find when you reach the top?
    You won't know unless you try!

When the Last Cloud's Past

What happens when the last cloud's past
    To reveal the bright full moon?
Does it portend clear skies ahead
    Or a new storm coming soon?
When will the last wave hit the beach,
    The ocean's constant pounding cease?
Will there ever be a time
    When all on earth know peace?
Who will be the person
    To think one last thought of hate?
Can you change your way of thinking
    Or is it much too late?

For as the waves bear down again
    And press on waiting sands
You have the answer to that question
    Right there in your hands.
Now that the final cloud has passed
    What will the heavens do?
Look inside your heart and mind
    For that depends on you.

What happens when the last cloud's past
    And reveals the clear night sky?
Is that a sight for all to see
    Or should we, to some, deny?
When will the mist all melt away,
    The land no more to haunt?
Will those with blindness see again
    And the hungry have no want?
What kind of person does it take
    To say they just don't care?
Are God's gifts so paltry, poor,
    That we refuse to share?
For as the mist retreats to sea
    And from the land does fade,
It becomes apparent
    That by His hands we all are made.
And if the last cloud passes on,
    What will the moonlight find?
May it be a person blessed
    Who blesses all in kind.

When the final cloud has passed,
    The moon's bright light revealed,
What appeared as barren ground
    Shines as fertile field.
When then, will leaves show bud
    And blossom on the tree?

Will there ever be a time
    When all on earth live free?
What kind of person does it take
    To make another slave?
For when we each are judged
    Won't it be by what we gave?
For the promise of the budding leaves
    Is spring, a life that's new,
And if freedom is to grow like that
    It must start with you.
Just as the last cloud passes
    Heaven showers us with light!
Would that we should use it here,
    On earth, to set things right.

Will you see the last cloud pass
    And the stars that shine above?
And if you do will you share
    The wonders of God's love?
Will you live to see the dawn,
    That grand rising of the sun?
Can you make it through the night
    Just by the deeds you've done?
And if God reached out to touch you
    Would you leap for joy and shout?
He's more sure than any sunrise
    To erase the clouds of doubt!
In dark of night or light of day
    Be you certain that He sees us,
For the promise of a brighter dawn
    Is the gift of life through Jesus.
For when the last clouds pass on life
    You'll be redeemed by just one deed—
Jesus gave His life for yours—
    With that alone, you're freed!

While I Wait, I Run

There's fire in the eastern sky
    But the hills still hide the sun.
I must wait to see its glory
    But while I wait, I run.
For there is light enough to see
    In the dark before the dawn,
And as long as I have air to breathe
    I will carry on.
This will be a day like all
    Filled with joy and sorrow,
And I must run today
    For I do not know tomorrow.
The clouds are disappearing,
    They give way to clearing skies,
But I will still be running
    When I see the sun arise.
There is no time for standing
    For there is work that must be done,
And God is calling me right now
    So while I wait, I run.

Five

Five points upon a star,
    Five fingers on my hand,
Of all that's in the universe
    Which of these, most grand?
A star, a mighty furnace
    That spreads its heat and light;
My hand that chooses destiny
    To do what's wrong or right.
A star so far and distant
    That I can only see;
My hand right here beside you
    Connecting you and me.

Such power in a star,
    It fills us all with awe,
But still it takes a hand
    So together we may draw.
Those who know the stars
    Can guide you on your way,
But those who use their hands
    Can lift them up to pray.
And in that instant—Glory!—
    His Spirit touches from afar,
And in my tiny hand He puts
    All the power of a star!

Sail the Rainbow

Far out on the horizon
    Rising from clouds and mist,
A rainbow arches in its splendor
    For a moment to exist.
All God's brilliance in one brush
    Of multicolored dye
Reflected by the ocean
    As it lights the evening sky.
Sail into the rainbow
    At the edges of the sea
And up into the stars
    In your journey to be free.
For like the sudden rainbow
    Life's glory is but short,
And your days will not be lengthened
    By the safety of this port.
Taste its every color,
    Feel its vibrant glow,
Ever onward, upward,
    As you sail the great rainbow.

Shining through the Rain

Cold and shivering, damp and dark,
    Body, soul, just like the day,
"God, please intervene for me
    And send this rain away!"
And yet it's pouring down on me
    Even heavier than before,
"I asked you, Lord, to make it stop,
    Why do You send me more?"
I need to know His answer
    So I look up to the skies,
And there I find my God's reply
    Revealed before my eyes.
A beacon shines from heaven
    Straight into my soul!
The God of all the universe
    Made, just for me, a hole.
I feel my Father's love for me
    And it soothes away my pain,
For Jesus, like a beam of light,
    Comes shining through the rain!

Chapter Two

Barefoot on Roses

Barefoot on Roses

I walk barefoot on the roses
  But I do not feel the thorn;
The thorns were banished from the earth
  On the day that you were born.
I walk barefoot on the grass
  But don't shy from the morning dew,
For I have felt naught but warm
  From the moment I met you.
I walk barefoot up the mountain
  But do not feel the stone,
For the love that fills my heart
  Gives me strength as yet unknown.
I walk barefoot on the beach
  But the sand will never burn;
I thank you for your gift of love,
  Much more than I could earn.
I walk barefoot through this life
  With sorrow forever banned
Because I'm touching you, my love,
  And we're walking hand in hand.

The Rose-Red Snow at Sunrise

I dreamt of you throughout the night,
    I could not sleep at dawn,
And rose this winter's morning
    With much to think upon.
And as I looked outside my window,
    Much to my surprise,
The snow appeared red as a rose
    As the sun pierced the morning skies.
It fills my heart with courage,
    This natural valentine,
And if I could pass it on to you
    Would you say that you'd be mine?
For I will give to you my everything,
    My whole heart and mind,
With nothing but a simple hope:
    You'd return my love in kind.
Yes, our love will be as pure
    As new fallen winter snows,
Yet with passion deep and lovely
    And all the sweetness of a rose.

Yesterday's Snow Is Gone

Yesterday's snow is gone
    And the skies are clearest blue;
The sun is shining once again
    Because, dear, I found you.
The winds that blew so harshly
    And chilled me to the bone
Have faded to a gentle breeze,
    The sweetest I have known.
The morning air is crisp and clean,
    The day has never been so bright;

My heart once lost in darkness
 Now fills with love's pure light.
Yes, the snow is gone forever,
 Such a difference in one day,
And all is well, for you're with me,
 Forevermore to stay.

Picnic by the River

A picnic and a blanket
 Set by the slowly moving river,
Here is where love's arrow struck,
 Taken fresh from Cupid's quiver.
I did not see him lurking
 As we feasted there and drank,
But I felt his arrow pierce my heart
 Here, on the river bank.
And I look into your eyes
 Hoping what I see is true,
That Cupid's arrow found its mark
 And then he aimed for you.
The world around has faded
 As side by side we lie,
Aware only of each other
 While the waters pass us by.
What a feeling to be so lost,
 Yet found there in your eyes,
For I would give it all for you
 With our love the only prize.

Dinner by Candlelight

Alone at last together
 At a table set for two,
Candlelight enough to see
 My only one is you.

We sit and talk and laugh
    And wander through this meal,
Yet I wonder how to tell you
    That true love is what I feel.
Reflecting flames of candlelight
    Perhaps my eyes will show it;
I say, "I love you"—and they have!—
    For you already know it.
And you love me too, my dear,
    Far beyond my wildest dreams,
Brighter than any candle
    The love we share now beams.
The feelings overwhelm me,
    Almost more than I can handle,
Love to light the darkest room
    As I blow out the candle.

Dance in the Moonlight

Come now, darling, dance with me
    Beneath the starlit skies,
And the beauty of the moon will tell
    What words can't vocalize.
For our love is like no other
    Throughout the galaxy,
And no sun or moon shines brighter
    Than this love 'tween you and me
The moonlight in your upturned eyes
    Shall the universe entrance,
And I am lost without you—
    Please come with me to dance!
And now we move together,
    Never more shall we alight,
For our love will take us far beyond
    The boundaries of flight.

So hold me close, don't let me go,
    Forever would be too soon,
And dance with me through time and space
    On the stairway to the moon.

Touched by a Rose Petal

Smooth as silk against my skin
    Like a feather floats in air,
Its fragrance washes clean my mind
    And soothes away each care.
The rose, a symbol of our love,
    So gentle to the touch,
Its beauty to be shared by two,
    For true love is made of such.
Beneath the rose's petals
    We two now meet as one,
And our love will grow more beautiful
    Like a rose in summer sun.
A single petal touched my face,
    It touches yours as well,
To draw us even closer still
    As time will surely tell.

Raindrops and Kisses

"Come with me to catch a raindrop!"
    You laughed and called to me,
And though I did not comprehend
    Now I clearly see.
For as we catch the raindrops
    They soak us through and through
So I cannot tell which ones I've caught
    And which belong to you.

And as the falling raindrops
    Cover tree and field
The beauty of God's plan for us
    Is suddenly revealed.
For we catch much more than water
    Falling through the air,
It's a loving kiss from heaven
    That we completely share.
For actions speak more clearly
    Than words can e'er explain,
And my answer is "Forever!"
    As you kiss me in the rain.

I Love You in the Summer Rain

The sun shines down through cotton clouds,
    There's a special glow about this place,
Yet dims next to my heart's delight:
    The sunshine of your face.
The birds are chirping merrily
    As they dart from tree to tree,
But it's the sound of your sweet laughter
    That brings heaven's joys to me.
I feel the warmth of raindrops
    And smell the sweetness of the land,
Yet such will never fill my heart
    As when you touch my hand.
I love you in the summer rain
    That sparkles in the mist
And settles gently on the rose
    As with a diamond it were kissed.
Oh, that we could share this day again
    In heavenly refrain,
For I will love you always, just as now,
    Here, in the summer rain.

A Simple Place for Love to Start

It should have been a ballroom
    As we walked across the floor
Or as I stormed the castle
    To throw down the tower door.
Such a place is sure and certain
    To unlock a lover's heart.
Why did we choose this simple place
    For our true love to start?
No wealth or earthly riches
    To our union did I bring.
How did we grow a love like ours
    From such a simple thing?
For when I look into your eyes
    I see all the treasure of this world,
And you say you see your shining knight
    Ride out with flags unfurled.
Our love began so simply
    And it simply stayed that way
And I will simply treasure you
    Forever, if I may.

Just One Star

Just one star in all the heavens
    Like a diamond in the night,
One star my only vision,
    One star my only light.
Just one flower in the garden,
    Such beauty it bestows,
A barren field made bountiful
    Graced by a single rose.
I hold it to my ear,
    The single shell upon the shore,

The voice inside that calls
   "Come with me, I'll show you more."
I follow where it leads me
   To see if it is true—
It is!—For here in all the world
   My only one is you.
Just one star in all the heavens,
   One shell in all the sea,
You're the flower that's most beautiful
   And the only one for me.

One Kiss for All the Roses

I offer you a yellow rose
   To catch the sun's bright rays,
But it's the laughter of your heart
   That adds sparkle to my days.
I offer you a pure white rose,
   Like silver snow, so soft,
For as snowflakes ride upon the breeze
   So love keeps us aloft.
I offer you a sweet pink rose,
   Luxurious, inviting,
For it's the chance to be with you
   That makes my life exciting.
I offer you a deep red rose
   To symbolize my heart,
For it is yours as well
   As this new life we start.
I offer you one single kiss
   For a rose of every hue,
One kiss for all the roses
   As I give my love to you.

For my mother, Marjorie, on her birthday

Chapter Three

I'll Still Fly

I'll Still Fly

Too dark to see the sun,
  Only clouds of grey,
Not dark enough for night
  Or light enough for day.
And I wander upwards
  Looking for the light,
Afraid to go straight forward,
  Turn left or go on right.
I feel you more than see you,
  Darting through the air,
But your movement gives me hope
  And energy to dare.
I lift my feet and raise my eyes,
  Such strength your courage brings!
And I will fly today as well,
  God, just give me wings!
For even though the skies were dark
  You found a way to fly,
And as God does lift me up,
  Come what may, then so shall I.

If I Crash

"It's too far a reach," they say,
    "Such a trip cannot succeed."
But I will try in spite of such,
    For I must do this deed.
All I am and hope to be
    I'll put in this one flight,
And though odds are stacked against me
    I'll try with all my might.
If all goes well you'll hear of me
    And the world will know my name,
And if I crash I'll light the skies
    With the brightest burning flame.
But do not mourn or sorrow
    If such should come to be,
For I would light the darkness
    And show the way for all to see.
And if I crash, what final thought
    Will I take with me as I die?
That God has given wings at last!
    And with them I'll still fly!

Written January 16, 2003 and dedicated as a memorial to the crew of the space shuttle
Columbia by the Scouts and Scouters of Troop 387 on February 8, 2003.

Vapor Trails

A noble mission taken
    With human bodies frail,
Now nothing left to see
    But a shining vapor trail.
The best of us they sought,
    So strong in mind and heart;
Our dreams, just like the ship they flew,
    Were quickly torn apart.

On a winter's morning
    They lit the azure sky.
The return we thought to celebrate
    Had sadly gone awry.
The vapor trail once narrow,
    Now scattered and dispersed,
And in silence we all mourned
    For those who suffered worst.
In parking lots and pastures
    On roofs and schoolyard grounds,
People do their best to help
    And our hope somehow rebounds.
We resolve not to be deterred
    By the errors that were made,
And more vapor trails will fill the sky
    Before winds cause these to fade.
For though we suffer setbacks
    We will not ever fail
If we follow these brave seven
    And their shining vapor trail.

For the crew of the shuttle Columbia

Our Outstretched Wings

Touching tips of wings
    Gliding on the air,
Two eagles soar together,
    A sight so grand and rare.
They reach the highest heights
    And disappear from view,
Yet they are still together
    Somewhere in the blue.
And should one eagle falter
    The other gives it lift,

The same as in our friendship,
     That rare and godly gift.
Like eagles with our wings outstretched
     Joined by touch of feather,
We rise o'er every obstacle
     Because we fly together.
So do not let what faces you
     Take your eyes off of the sky,
For an eagle gives its brother lift
     And so, my friend, do I.

For my brother in Christ, Rogers Hazel

The Eagle Rises

Farther than the eye can see
     Does the noble eagle rise,
And though the air's too thin to breathe,
     Still the eagle flies.
The earth is far below him now
     But his gaze is skyward still.
Where blood and feathered wing have failed
     He journeys on his will.
And though he's traveled far beyond
     The limits of my sight,
I will remember and retell
     This eagle's gallant flight.
He slipped the bonds of earth
     And touched the very stars;
So follow him we may and must,
     For the next set of wings is ours.
For as long as we shall live
     Our ears will hear his cry
Calling us to try those wings
     And set our targets high.

For the courage of such birds and men
    Our spirit energizes
As up into the hand of God
    The noble eagle rises.

Suggested by Robert Krammer as a memorial to William McCool,
Eagle Scout and copilot of the Columbia

Chapter Four

Footsteps in the Garden

Footsteps in the Garden

A shuffled foot, an easy laugh,
　　There are footsteps in the garden
To celebrate last week's parade,
　　The one that Jesus starred in.
Softly now we speak
　　And talk of what's to be:
Peace on earth for everyone,
　　A certain victory.
So sure we are that all is well
　　We soon fall fast asleep,
But there is One who carries on,
　　His promises to keep.
Would that we had heeded Him
　　When He gave us call,
Jesus, God's only Son,
　　Who lived to save us all.
A footstep in the garden,
　　A sandal on a stone,
Jesus, the One and only,
　　Now stands guard alone.

A snapping stick, an angry shout,
　　There are footsteps in the garden,

Even blessed with Jesus' love
    How human hearts can harden!
Fiercely now the voices raise
    And with them rock and fist,
"This man is not as one of us!
    Do not allow Him to exist!"
In an instant all is lost,
    My Master's gone away,
And I cannot ever save Him now,
    No matter what I pray.
The crowds that cheered now mock Him
    And the blood runs in his eyes;
Alone now on a cross of wood
    My Lord Jesus dies.
No footsteps in the garden,
    Just a bloody stone,
For the Son of God was made like me
    Of human flesh and bone.

"Hosanna in the highest!"
    There are footsteps in the garden!
Rejoice now one and all,
    For Jesus has won pardon.
Hear the angels singing
    And join their happy chorus;
Jesus died and rose again
    And He did it all for us!
Who has eyes to see?
    Who has ears to hear?
Jesus has defeated death
    And there's nothing left to fear.
Yes, I too will heed Him now
    For I have a second chance;
What He's offered me is yours as well
    So join me in the dance!

Joyous footsteps in the garden
    And happy, dancing feet
To celebrate Christ's holy gift
    And victory complete!

One Strong Heart

Two eyes to see earth's beauty,
    Two ears to hear her sounds,
Two hands to do the miracles
    And show how love abounds.
A mouth and tongue to tell the way
    And His wisdom to impart;
Yet all of them depend like us
    On Jesus' one strong heart.

Two nails to stretch His arms,
    One to hold His feet,
Two criminals to die beside,
    His loss was so complete.
They took Him from the cross
    And laid Him in the street,
But in the hidden tomb
    One strong heart began to beat!

Two births for every Christian,
    For the body and the soul,
Born to die yet live again,
    For Jesus paid the toll.
Fill my heart now, Jesus,
    In Your holy name I pray,
For in my chest, dear Savior,
    My heart beats for You, today.

Come Away

Come away by yourselves to a lonely place,
    Come away, my friends, and rest;
Take the time you need today,
    Don't rush back to take the test.
Sorrow has found you and brought you down,
    Now to yourselves you must be kind,
And through rest and contemplation
    May you some comfort find.
You have lost so very much
    And things are not the same,
But the tears you shed are noble ones
    And in them there's no shame.
Come away, my friends, and be with me,
    I will give you comfort there,
And perhaps we'll find a smile or two
    In the fellowship we share.
There is nothing that we can do
    Yet there is much to say,
And I will bear your sorrows
    If you'll just come away.

Always Watch Me

I was in such a quandary,
    Lost beyond all aid,
I finally turned to Jesus
    And this is what I prayed:
"Lord, I don't know what to do
    Though I've pondered long and deep.
How can I know what thoughts to lose
    And which ones I'm to keep?"
I listened for an answer,
    A truth that was the key,

And Jesus gave me His reply,
    "Just keep your eyes on Me.
Do not look beyond My face
    Or try the limits of your sight,
For I will be the one to watch
    And I will make things right."
And that which had been cloudy
    Now becomes at once quite clear:
With Jesus living in my heart
    There is naught to fear.
And if they accuse me wrongly
    I can turn the other cheek
And use His words, not mine,
    For it's His message that I speak.
I do not have to answer
    Or make a plan to win,
For when I need a good reply
    The Spirit comes again.
There is One whom I must answer to
    And it's not you or them;
Jesus is the One I need
    And I'll be watching Him!

A Different Race

He won the race in record time
    According to the judges' clocks,
So they made him run the second heat
    Without using starter's blocks.
"We really fixed him this time,"
    They laughed as he started late,
But he caught them at the halfway point
    And passed them all by the final gate.

"He must be cheating to run like that,
     We know it can't be right!"
They made him race again with weights
     And blinders to block his sight.
They made him run in a narrow lane
     Where his feet could hardly fit.
There were chains around his ankles, too,
     But he won in spite of it.
No cheers to greet him past the line,
     Just jeers and angry groans.
They didn't crown him champion,
     Instead they pummeled him with stones.

As he lay in silent agony,
     The crowd quietly filed out;
They'd put this challenge down for good,
     Of that they had no doubt.
"He's dead I tell you," they all laughed,
     "Let's just leave his body there.
Even if he lives,
     To run again, he'll never dare."
His body was badly broken,
     He didn't run for many years,
And even when he finally healed
     He couldn't race for all his fears.
His heart grew angry at those fears
     For it knew that he could win,
But where to go for courage
     To run that race again?
He searched deep and far for answers
     And finally found the only one,
A man who died upon a cross
     Yet rose again: God's only Son.

Yes, Jesus suffered on that cross
    With each painful dying breath,
Yet in the greatest race of all,
    Jesus won, and He beat death.
Just as Jesus raised Himself to life
    He picked that runner off the floor;
Now with Jesus in his heart
    The runner dared to race once more.
The crowd was set against him
    As the race was about to start,
But their evil no longer frightened him
    For he had Jesus in his heart.
His body had recovered all
    And he ran an awesome pace;
At last the crowd was silenced
    When he once more won the race.
For this time they could not stop him,
    No matter what they tried,
Since Jesus ran beside him
    And matched his every stride.

A Shelter in the Rock

High atop the mountain
    Just below the peak,
A mighty rock, split in two,
    Provides the shelter that we seek.
What force it must have taken
    To rend this giant stone
So we could have a place to rest
    Our weary flesh and bone.
And as we settle down to sleep
    Now safe from wind and rain,

I think about the risen Christ
    Who on a cross was slain.
A hammer on a nail
    And through Jesus' hand, a hole,
And in that mighty rock I find
    A shelter for my soul.
He hung upon a cross of death
    That nail driven through his hand,
A hole that opened heaven's gate
    And a rock on which to stand.

The Forgotten Gift

He put it on his Christmas list
    When he was just a boy,
And he prayed to Jesus often,
    For this gift was not a toy.
For many years he sought it,
    But it was never there,
And sometimes he grew bitter;
    It just did not seem fair.
There were many things to do,
    The boy became a man;
The gift he asked for he forgot
    But Jesus had a plan.
"Lose your life for Me,
    Treat others as yourself,"
When the man had done these things
    His gift came off the shelf.
And now he walks in wonder,
    A smile of joy upon his face.
He got the gift he asked for:
    Jesus gave him grace.

Hope for a Heartbeat

When all the doors are closed
   And every room is dark,
When hope is lost forever,
   Lord, You provide that spark.
For an instant I can see
   A single point of light;
Oh, send Your Holy Spirit, Lord,
   My spirit to ignite.
Jesus, light the way for me,
   Enough so I can cope,
You and You alone, my Lord,
   Are the heartbeat of my hope.

Lord, you give me:
One heartbeat of hope,
   Courage so I can pray,
Seek mercy for a minute
   And help throughout the day.
Jesus, be my Savior
   And help me on my climb,
Love me, Lord, for all my life
   Beyond the end of time.

My burden's heavy, Lord,
   I carry too much sin.
Won't you take them for a minute
   E'er I pick them up again?
Can it be so easy?
   I have too much to confess,
Jesus, it's impossible,
   That Your answer would be "Yes!"
Relief for just an instant,
   Your mercy for a minute,

Yet unexpected, undeserved,
 Find compassion infinite.

Lord, you give me:
One heartbeat of hope,
 Courage so I can pray,
Seek mercy for a minute
 And help throughout the day.
Jesus, be my Savior
 And help me on my climb;
Love me, Lord, for all my life
 Beyond the end of time.

Like leaves in spring Your gifts appear,
 More plentiful than rain,
Your love renews my broken life
 And washes off the pain.
A little love is all I need,
 Of Your garment just one touch,
Your love so overwhelms me, Lord,
 Boundless! Oh, so much!
Completely filled, yet more I seek;
 Daily send it from above
So I can share with others
 A lifetime of Your love.

Lord, you give me:
One heartbeat of hope,
 Courage so I can pray,
Seek mercy for a minute
 And help throughout the day.
Jesus, be my Savior
 And help me on my climb;
Love me, Lord, for all my life
 Beyond the end of time.

Hope for a heartbeat,
    Mercy for a minute,
A lifetime of Your love,
    Full, now that You are in it!
With You as my Savior,
    To heaven's heights I'll climb!
Loving You as You've loved me,
    Beyond the end of time.

The Three-Word Gospel

F
R
E
E
J E S<u>US</u>!

Chapter Five

The Sound of Freedom's Sail

The Sound of Freedom's Sail

I can hear her in the cheering crowds
    As she marks the Fourth of July
Even with the fireworks
    Exploding in the sky.
Above the roar of crashing waves,
    In the stiffest ocean gale,
Snapping in the wind,
    She is freedom's billowed sail.
With open eyes I look to her,
    The red, the white and blue,
Yet even in the darkest night
    Her sounds keep coming through,
Calling loudly, "One and all,
    Never be afraid!
March beside the Stars and Stripes
    In freedom's grand parade!"

With sounds of battle crashing
    And the din of falling shells,
Through her torn and tattered weeping
    Her agony she tells.
She cries for all her children,
    The noble and the brave,

Who knew the cost of freedom
    Yet, for us all, they gave.
With moistened eyes I'm blinded,
    But I can hear her still
Standing guard for those who lie
    Beneath this sacred hill.
Calling softly, "Everyone!
    Remember each brave soul.
To live in peace and freedom
    Should also be your goal."

I hear her every morning
    Above the trumpet call
In the softly rustling breeze
    That touches one and all.
And she calls me in the evening
    As the sun begins to set,
Though taken down and folded
    She's not through talking yet.
I close my eyes and touch her
    And hold her to my chest.
Of all the flags I've ever held
    This one is the best,
Whispering to me, "All is well.
    You are safe with me.
When you hear me calling in the wind
    Take heart! For you are free!"

On the Fringe

The stars each mean a state;
    The blue is loyalty.
The white is clean and noble;
    The red, blood of the free.

And what of all this fringe,
　　The gold upon the edge?
It's like people who don't listen
　　When they say our nation's pledge.
They really like the honor,
　　And to the flag they cling,
But they do not mean the words
　　In the anthems that they sing.
The flag can do without them
　　For it stands upon its own.
Are you a real part of the flag
　　Or just some fringe that it has grown?
Do you understand what freedom means
　　Like the red, the white and blue?
Then you will defend America
　　When she depends on you.

Where Freedom Lives

Freedom lives on playgrounds as children run and play;
　　Freedom lives in a sculptor's hands
　　　　That mold a piece of clay.
I see freedom in a lecture hall as students come to learn
　　And in a baseball game as each batter waits his turn.
Freedom lives on oceans wide, in walks on sun-soaked sand;
　　Freedom lives in America, for God has blessed this land.

Freedom lives in words we write and in the things we say;
　　Freedom lives because of God, and it's to Him we pray.
There is freedom choosing where to live and in what job to do;
　　There's freedom when you speak a thought,
　　　　Especially when it's true.
Freedom lives inside our minds, in words and actions grand;
　　Freedom lives in America, for God has blessed this land.

Freedom lives in dark of night, in light before the dawn;
    Freedom lives in all our lives, and we must pass it on.
There was freedom at the Commons
      And freedom at the bridge;
    There was freedom when they raised the flag
      High atop that ridge.
Freedom lives and prospers when people make their stand;
    Freedom lives in the U.S.A., for God has blessed this land.

Freedom lives like holy fire, the torch cannot go out!
    Freedom lives forever, in us there is no doubt.
There is freedom in a spaceship that goes to moon or Mars;
    There is freedom in a dream that reaches past the stars.
Freedom is a gift to us given by God's hand,
    And freedom lives in America, for He has blessed this land!

With the Seasons

It seems the same.
The birds are calling.
People walk their dogs.
No one speaks of it.
We nod in passing
On our Sunday jogs.
First spring weekend,
Beautiful,
Just breathing is a joy.
But tomorrow,
What will tomorrow bring?
This planet to destroy?
Wars we've had before;
It's in the heart of man.
But they seek to kill us all
And they'll do it if they can.
With the seasons
Time moves on.

There is no backward going.
It seems so peaceful here
But now
There is no knowing.
And even if
I hide my eyes
And try to look away,
My mind still sees the pictures
And it does my heart betray.

First of spring
And first of war,
I can see the road ahead:
Pain and suffering,
Agony,
Too many people dead.
Tomorrow's history books
Will say
We had to try
For the evil that pursues us
Would have us all to die.
I pray that in a future spring
Someone else will sit and write,
Free to breathe and think
As I try to do tonight.

Just One Hundred

A hundred men and women
    (The highways do much more)
Seems like a small price to pay
    For what we're fighting for.
Just a hundred soldiers
    Who sacrificed it all,
And several hundred thousand more
    Who answered freedom's call.

Such a tiny number
    Compared to World War II,
But would it seem so little
    If one of those were you?
Just a hundred soldiers
    With dreams and goals like me
And futures bright and promising
    That they will never see.
Children without parents
    And some who'll never be,
One hundred priceless lives—
    The cost of being free.

Three Scouts Left

Three men gather at the grave
    Remembering the cheer they gave,
Clapping hands, four, five times now,
    Odd that they can still know how.
Hands that moved so slow before,
    How can this their youth restore?
Mourners hear them clap and shout,
    Wonder, "What's this all about?"
Quick and sharp, the hands grow loud,
    They give their all to make him proud.
Am I blinded by the sun?
    Or is it boys there having fun?
Hiking, camping, these they did,
    But time these boys, like others, hid.
Listen now! What do you hear?
    Youthful voices in this cheer!
Three old men I saw before,
    Boy Scouts again—and there are four.

In honor of the Scouts of Troop 20, University Presbyterian Church, Austin, Texas, who as boys formed lifetime friendships

---

Chapter Six

Stained Glass Garden Window

Stained Glass Garden Window

To every flower, every leaf,
  It gives a different hue;
It anticipates the spring
  And helps that dream come true.
It reminds me that this winter,
  Like all those before, will pass,
And that when the roses bloom
  I won't need this colored glass.
Free to walk in wonder
  Through the garden God has made,
The colors then so bountiful
  To fill this little glade.
And I think upon my window
  When the times I face are tough,
Remembering that—like the glass—
  A dream can be enough
To sustain a person's hopes
  While God's garden grows,
Our answered prayers astounding
  Like the blooming of the rose.

Thomas Dowden

It was on an application
    The lad reversed his name
And realized that in his mind
    And heart he felt the same.
"I need proof," he thought,
    "If I trust, you might just lie.
How is it He could rise again?
    It's over when you die.
He'll have to hold His hands out
    For me to touch and see."
And so began the journey
    Of doubtin' Thomas D.

His mother made him go to church
    But he couldn't hide his sneers;
When his sister sang in children's choir
    He covered both his ears.
They all went to Grandma's house
    Each Thanksgiving day,
And she surprised her grandson
    When she asked Thomas to pray.
"Grandma, I don't think that Jesus
    Wants to hear a prayer from me,
'Cause if He's real He knows my heart
    And I'm doubtin' Thomas D."

His grandma cocked her head
    And peered into his eyes.
"Thomas," she said, "You're at that age
    And this is no surprise.
There are things that you're unsure of
    And we must have a talk,

So humor an old woman
    And join me for a walk.
Dear Thomas, I think that Jesus
    And I would both agree
Now's the time to speak your heart
    'Cause I'm certain Granny D.!"

They talked of many things, these two:
    The child she lost at birth,
The sorrow that she felt the day
    They put his grandpa in the earth.
Yet it wasn't sadness that he saw in her
    For her face was bright with joy,
And as the Spirit filled her up
    She reached out and touched the boy.
'Twas Jesus' hands he felt and saw,
    And he fell down to his knees.
She knelt, and side by side they prayed,
    Now, two certain D's.

Jesus knows your heart and mind,
    But the choice is up to you.
So when the clouds of doubt swirl round
    What are you going to do?
Will you try to hide it
    And store it up inside?
For 'tis an ancient struggle
    'Tween His love, your pride.
Will it take a vision
    To finally set you free?
Then look into the face of love
    Like doubtin' Thomas D.

Irish Soda Bread

She rises ere the sun
    Creeps through kitchen window panes
And makes enough for all her guests,
    Yet a little bit remains.
So after they've had breakfast,
    Some casual, friendly talk,
She takes the crumbs and slices
    To toss out on the walk.
The birds are there to greet her,
    For it's a regular routine,
And like the kitchen platters
    The sidewalk's soon picked clean.
She laughs to see their eagerness;
    They tarry in hopes of more.
She shakes her head and laughs again
    And goes back through the door.
She's happy that her winged friends
    And guests are wholly fed,
For it's more than meal, it's love she puts
    In Irish soda bread.

For my friend and fellow Optimist, Dr. Ty Winter

More Than Ever

It wasn't done by magic
    Or by Cupid's special arrow,
But the songs I heard were sweeter
    Than any robin, jay, or sparrow.
I didn't have to search
    Or sail the ocean blue,
For whenever I needed love
    I just looked to you.

And you were always there
    To kiss an injured knee
And to warn me of the perils
    That I could not yet see.
I did not always listen
    And that hurt you some I know,
But you taught me well and let me learn
    And gave me room to grow.
Yes, I've sailed the oceans now
    And seen many distant lands
As I have grown and changed
    From that baby in your hands.
And the love that's in my heart,
    It also changed and grew,
And I mean it more than ever, Mom,
    When I say that I love you!

Light Friendly Snows

I see them falling softly,
    Flakes so big and white,
To make a dreary winter's day
    Into a pretty sight.
Not enough to fill the streets
    Or to shovel off the walk,
So I make a cup of coffee
    And we settle down to talk.
Our voices soft as falling snow
    With peaceful thoughts as well;
Light friendly snows today,
    I'm really glad you fell.
There are just so many moments
    And time alone's so rare,
And this friendly snow today
    Gave us some to share.

Stone Pillars

Stone pillars on a vacant lot,
  A house and home that time forgot;
Alone now on this empty space
  I must now my failure face:
Expectations far too great,
  A young man fallen from their weight.
An older man with weary eyes
  Looks for help from distant skies.
The young man called, it never came;
  The old man fears the very same.
With fading hope he draws each breath
  And looks afar, beyond his death.
With words he travels quick through time,
  To the stars he seeks to climb.
The old man feared the young man dead
  But lived in long lost dreams instead.
The expectations are long past
  But he fulfills them, now, at last.

Castles in the Sand

We took our shoes off by the water
  To run barefoot on the beach,
For the sand was cool and clean
  Far as the eye could reach.
We swam in ocean waters,
  Built castles in the sands,
Brought bread to feed the seagulls
  And they ate it from our hands.
We saw the sailboats drifting,
  We watched the red sun set;
Though tides washed down our castles
  The day we won't forget.

We crossed the dunes together
    Singing, hand in hand,
Touched by ocean breezes,
    Barefoot in the sand.

All That's Left

The house is quiet, empty now,
    The kids and grandkids gone;
He walks into the kitchen
    And puts the kettle on.
Every day for fifty years
    He's followed this routine,
It's shriek their fathomed signal
    "Time now to convene."
They'd sit and talk together
    In regards to that and this;
Her smile to start his day
    Is the thing that he'll most miss.
Her earthly body's buried now
    But he feels her spirit near;
He takes a sip of coffee
    And wipes away a tear.
He'll go out to the grocery store,
    Talk to family on the phone;
He'll try to make her proud of him
    And make it on his own.
Each day before they parted
    These two held hands in prayer,
And he puts his hand across the table
    As if she still were there.
He cries now, uncontrollably,
    For his heart is cruelly cleft;
One plus one was more than two,
    But now, he's all that's left.

Grandma's Gardenias

They weren't like the other flowers
    That were gathered on that day,
And in colors they were far outshined
    By every other spray.
For the buds had not yet opened
    Nor any petal shown,
Yet the gardenias were the ones she chose
    To take home and call her own.
She knew the roots were bound
    So she bought a bigger pot,
Brought them in when it was cold,
    And watered them a lot.
And all at once they blossomed,
    There are twelve on every stem,
For she poured in all the love
    That she had given him.
Her love flowered in gardenias,
    Children, grandkids, too,
In church and in community
    That love keeps pouring through.
It was only one small basket
    She took home that day,
But, like her love, they keep on growing
    With every bit she gives away.

To my mother-in-law Alyene Pierot

Puddles by the Roses

He bathes the roses early
    As the sun creeps through the trees,
But tears roll down his cheeks—
    What is it that he sees?
For the roses are in bloom,
    Their beauty beyond measure,

Does he cry in awe of elegance
    Or has he lost some priceless treasure?
Perhaps he's the one who's gone astray,
    For a pond is forming at his feet;
The curb becomes a waterfall
    Pouring over on the street.
Finally he notices,
    Wipes the tears that streak his face,
Turns the water off,
    And puts the hose back in its place.
What is it that he's looking for
    As he tears out every weed?
The garden was her pride and joy
    And not an inch will he concede.
He remembers rising with the dawn
    Just a few short weeks ago;
The sun shined down on her alone,
    But she made his whole world glow.
So that is why he weeps
    As he gives the garden special care,
And there are puddles by the roses
    Because he sees her there.

Last of the Season Run

I see the buds; spring is near.
    There's a freshness in the air,
Yet I pull my sled to the hidden hill
    To see if snow's still there.
A soft white secret just for me
    Guarded well by rock and tree,
One last chance to feel the wind
    And the joy of running free.
This gift is mine today,
    For tomorrow I'm without,

So I will travel faster still—
    Just listen to me shout!
If on my arms I had wings
    I know that I could fly,
But my final run is over
    And it's time to say good-bye.
Sorry now to leave,
    But what a day it's been.
And when I wake up in the morning
    It'll be—today again!

Chapter Seven

Walter Wupperman's Wings

Walter Wupperman's Wings

They gathered along Texas Street
    From top to bottom of the hill,
And as Walter stepped out from the walk
    The crowd was hushed and still.
He was tall and skinny for his age
    With arms especially long;
He had flapped his wings for weeks
    To try to make them strong.
The bruises were still visible
    From his last aborted goof,
But his cardboard wings had padded him
    When he jumped off of the roof.
His wingspan was impressive
    As he turned into the wind,
And the crowd all held its breath
    As he started to descend.
Walter took those giant strides
    And flapped with all his might;
If trying could have given lift
    He would have taken flight.
When Walter reached the bottom
    His arms were tired and sore,

And his mother seemed relieved
    When he said, "I'll try no more!"
But everyone who watched him
    Has remembered to this day
The time that Walter Wupperman
    Tried to fly away.

Thinking Upside Down

I had a dream this morning
    And I think I was a bat—
'Cause I was hanging upside down!
    How can they think like that?
"Keep your feet off of the ceiling!"
    That's what my mother said,
"If you put your feet up
    Your blood all rushes to your head!"
So how is it that mother bats
    Have this lesson switched about?
For when you think upside down
    It creates odd looks and doubt!
We say that bats are batty,
    Their flight so unpredictable.
It's names like that we people use
    To make other's thoughts constrictable.
Yet a bat can catch ten thousand bugs
    And I can't swat a fly,
And if I'm thinking for myself
    I can figure out just why.
Yes, anyone who's different
    Is called a freak or clown,
But sometimes great advancements come
    From thinking upside down!

Leading the Unicorn

Free and wild, so beautiful,
    The unicorn fills my dreams.
What joy 'twould be to catch it!
    So close I am it seems.
And then it walks right up to me,
    The reins are in my hands.
It's freedom and its faith are mine
    As in front of me it stands.
With such power I am now endowed
    To lead it through the land,
But the dream that is the unicorn
    I do not yet understand.
For no matter how I try to lead
    I cannot avoid its horn,
And I cannot lead my dreams
    Anymore than this unicorn.
What then to do with this magic horse
    That gave itself to me?
I take the bridle from its mouth
    And let my dreams run free.
I touch the mystic horse of dreams
    And its strength I feel inside!
I am one now with my unicorn
    And where I go, I ride.

Hanging Stars and Planets

There's something I must tell you,
    A visit from last night:
An angel took me on a tour,
    A little sample flight.
It showed me many things
    That angels get to do

And bid me choose my favorite
    By the time that we were through.
I've always liked the rainbows,
    The sunsets, and the dawn,
But then there's spring and snowflakes…
    The list goes on and on.
And then it showed me angels
    Hanging stars way out in space;
They sought the darkest corner
    And put light into that place.
Then they put out planets
    To spin around that sun,
And I said, "That's the job for me,
    'Cause that sure looks like fun!"
And then my trip was over
    And I woke up in my bed,
Not far off in the cosmos,
    I'm here on earth instead.
But I don't have to ride a rocket
    Or journey just one mile,
For I can add some light
    When I make a person smile.
I don't have to wait for heaven,
    My godly task to do,
I can start today—right now!—
    And so, my friend, can you!

Lost and Found for Dreams

I lost a dream this morning
    And went searching through my brain,
For as I woke it faded
    Like chalk marks in the rain.
I found a man to help me
    At the lost and found for dreams;

He looked inside a box for it
    Underneath old stars and sunbeams.
"No," he said, "It's not here,
    Can you tell me where it led?
Did you follow it alone
    Or take another dream instead?
Was it really yours?
    Please tell me how you know.
Could it be another's dream
    They gave you long ago?
Did you put your name on it,
    Big so all could see,
So they could bring it back to you
    Instead of here to me?
Do you really want your dream?
    If not please go away,
For if you do not love your dream
    Let it go so someone may."

Russian Language Music

Russian thoughts of life and love
    In halting English wrest,
Melodic like a symphony
    In their native tongue expressed.
I close my eyes and listen
    And travel with the sounds.
The voice speaks words I do not know
    Yet in richness it abounds.
I feel the power, energy,
    As he speaks each word,
And I feel the meaning
    In the sounds that I have heard.
Am I dreaming of the time before
    Babel split asunder?

Russian language music flows
    And, God, it makes me wonder:
Are thoughts we think dictated
    By the language that we use,
Or are there words in every tongue
    To express the thoughts we choose?
Russian language music
    Half a world away,
Says we can work together
    And must do so every day.

El Emeno

Life is going by too fast;
    It seems that nothing can be slow.
As children we had a word for that:
    We called it "El Emeno."
El Emeno was powerful
    On very special days,
And it's El Emeno with our babies
    As they change quickly phase by phase.
I stay busy all the time;
    El Emeno makes me sick.
Whenever we are having fun,
    The clock is much too quick.
How did we get El Emeno?
    We heard it in a song:
We never could say L, M, N, and O,
    That simply took too long.
So next time you sing the alphabet,
    Sing it nice and slow
So your children will grow up
    Never knowing "El Emeno."

Glue

Helps to make a picture,
    Holds puzzles in their place,
Sticks two things together,
    Puts stars upon your face.
Be loyal to your friends
    And always say what's true;
Do the right thing every day
    And you won't be needing glue.

The Kettle, the Pot and What They Were Not

The pot thought the kettle was a bit too black;
The kettle looked at the pot and saw a crack.
Isn't it funny, they both had a knack
To see faults in the other without looking back?

The horse hates how the donkeys gather and bray;
The donkeys all sneer when they hear a neigh.
Neither will listen whatever they say,
And they both think that living like that is okay.

The cat thought the dog barked too loud;
The dog hated the cat for how it meowed.
Friendship between them they never allowed;
To forgive or forget they were much too proud.

You look at me in utter dismay,
And I wonder at your sorry display.
Each of us wishes the other away,
And we must each change that. Now! Today!

The black helped the kettle cook really hot;
In spite of the crack the pot held a lot.
Once each saw this, they anger forgot—
For both what they were and what they were not.

The Thread's View

As I settled down to sleep last night
    A thought intrigued my mind:
I wonder what a thread sees
    In the rug that it does bind.
Does it see the patterns
    That it, with others, weaves?
Or are such things, for a thread,
    Just something it believes?
And do the threads around it
    Laugh and give it grief,
Like Christians who profess their faith
    Are mocked for their belief?
But I can see the pattern,
    I have a broader view,
As God sees all the cosmos
    And I one single clue.
How to tell the thread
    Of the beauty that it makes?
God sent a thread named Jesus,
    And that is all it takes!
Like a thread I follow
    The path God's set for me,
On faith I know the pattern
    That one day soon, I'll see!

Fielder's Choice

It was in a children's pick up game
    On one of those rocky lots;
They were picking teams and who would play
    In all the fielding spots.
Everything had been taken,
    Then one child came in late,

"Sit down on the bench," they said,
    "You're going to have to wait!"
But one boy spoke up loud and clear,
    "I think we all should play,
Since the game is all in fun
    And we're not keeping score today."
His comments raised a clamor,
    "If he plays you'll have to sit!
You have to make that choice
    And there's no way out of it."
But the boy was calm as he replied
    (And there was firmness in his voice),
"I will consider all my options.
    You will NOT define my choice!
There are many things
    That I can choose to do,
And the last thing on my list
    Is to give it up to you!"
And as they took the field,
    Ten players versus nine,
I wondered what choices I had lost
    By letting someone else define.
So listen hard when someone tells you
    That you must pick which way to lose.
Stop and think! Then do what's right.
    It's the only way to choose!

Life of the Party

A plate of cookies, half eaten,
    Ice cream soft and runny,
Jokes that we all laughed at
    But don't know what made them funny.
Friends that thought enough of us
    To visit for an hour,

I'm too tired to clean it up right now
    Or even take a shower.
We planned so and we strategized
    To put this party on,
Yet as soon as it had started
    It seemed everyone was gone.
And how long will they remember
    The decorations, food, and drink?
Life's forgotten like a party,
    And much too short, I think.

Turnabout Mountain

"You've come far," the old man said, "I'd even say done well.
    But the final outcome's yet to be
      And what comes next will tell.
Cast your eyes into the sunset, to that highest mountain peak,
    For unless you reach the top
      You'll never gather what you seek.
Many have tried to pass that way, so many I quit countin',
    But most I see head back this way
      When they come to Turnabout Mountain."

The old man shook his head, admitted, "Yes, I too once tried.
    I almost made it to the top but then the oxen died.
A blizzard came howling from the north
    With twenty feet of snow.
    Least that's how I remember it, 'twas so long ago.
I'd go with you once again if it weren't for all this doubtin',
    Afraid that's the thing that happens
      When you turn back at Turnabout Mountain."

The old man turned about and peered into the west.
    I think he must have wondered if in truth he'd done his best.
But his words deepened our resolve that we would not be broken;

We made a promise with our eyes
    Though not a word was spoken.
For such a fellowship as ours there can be no accountin',
    It's all for one and one for all
        To conquer Turnabout Mountain.

The blizzards came, the oxen died,
    But we climbed while we had breath,
    For our resolve was "it or us"—we were in it to the death!
Each step was utter agony but it felt worse to stop,
    And because we climbed together we each made it to the top.
The dreams we had came true with blessings like a fountain!
    That's what happens when you stick it out
        In spite of Turnabout Mountain.

That was many years ago and now I too am old.
    All are gone who climbed with me
        And made that trip so bold.
Yet they live on in me and we'll live on in you,
    For when you see that distant peak
        We know what you will do.
Like us you'll brave the danger
        And we'll know it from the shoutin',
    That you have made it to the top
        And over Turnabout Mountain.

High on Heaven's Rope

Just one moment to be brave,
    Of courage, just a drop…
What is it that's within me
    That causes me to stop?
Just hold the rope and lift my feet,
    It all depends on me,
For I'm the one who's holding back
    My certain destiny.

I hear the voices calling out,
    "You can do it! Hurry! Go!"
"I'm going," say my lips,
    But my muscles still say, "No!"
I lift my eyes to heaven
    And the beauty of the sky,
My feet follow in an instant
    And free at last, I fly!
I hold the rope to heaven
    As over earth I swing,
With one drop of Jesus' courage
    I can do—anything!

For anyone who's ever swung on a rope swing,
and with special thanks to Malcolm and Patsy Williams and
Camp Country Lad, Monterey, Tennessee.

Chapter Eight

The Dead Snake's Bite

The Dead Snake's Bite

He dug it up. He had to see.
    He found the severed head.
He touched it unafraid,
    For it was clearly dead.
He laughed to think how scared he was
    When he heard its rattle near,
And put his finger in its mouth
    To prove he had no fear.
He felt his heartbeat quicken
    Though the snake could not attack;
He imagined it alive again,
    And drew his finger quickly back.
Alas! He touched the hanging tooth;
    His finger snagged and bled.
He felt the venom's vicious gnaw
    And then, in fear, he fled.
Though you win the battle,
    Taunting's never right;
When you dig up buried dangers
    Expect the dead snake's bite.

The Breath Holding Contest

Just three feet of water,
  Pretty hard to drown.
Who would need a breath first,
  And who would be the last one down?
Some came up in thirty seconds,
  Most in just a minute,
And fifteen seconds later
  Only two could win it.
They fought fire in their lungs
  To a minute forty-five,
Then one came up for air
  While the other took a dive.
They quickly pulled him out
  And laid him on the dock;
The lifeguards gave him CPR
  While the crowd all watched in shock.
Their turn now to choke a breath
  'Til he inhaled again,
And almost instantly he asked,
  "Tell me! Did I win?"
His pride had got the best of him,
  A nearly fatal blunder.
Do we learn from our mistakes?
  It gives me cause to wonder.

The Little Pyromaniac

He could always start a campfire
  With just a match or two,
And flames would climb to twenty feet
  Before that lad was through.
His father warned him many times
  That fire was really hot,

But, like too many boys these days,
    Listen he would not.
He found a can of gasoline
    High on a shelf, well hidden,
Got a ladder, brought it down,
    Though he knew it was forbidden.
He took it to the outhouse,
    Poured it down the pit,
"Eliminate the smell," he thought,
    "That'll be the end of it."
But when he tossed the match
    The entire outhouse blew!
It layered all the field
    And the little pyro, too.
Yes, he raised a stink that day,
    One skill that he could master.
Follow rules! Don't play with fire!
    Or you court your own disaster.

Sinbad and the Golden Horseshoes

The stallion stood at twenty hands,
    As best his men could measure.
They groomed his coat until it glowed,
    Now this was Sinbad's treasure.
A bridle laid with rubies,
    Silk ribbons to hold the braids,
For a thing so mighty and so great
    A man makes many trades.
Sinbad had been most crafty;
    He tricked and then he lied,
But he knew just what he wanted
    And would not be denied.
The stallion was so beautiful,
    So powerful and fleet,

And golden horseshoes Sinbad bought
    To place upon its feet.
Such a horse could never lose;
    Sinbad bet his fortune on a race,
But the gold was far too heavy
    And his horse gave up the chase.
Sinbad lost it all,
    The horse, the jewels, the gold;
He'd even bet his freedom,
    So into slavery he was sold.
Wealth can make you foolish
    And swell you up with pride,
But when the judgment comes
    It won't give you place to hide.
Don't wear the golden horseshoes
    Or like Sinbad be the fool,
But store your gold in heaven
    With Jesus, your only jewel.

Bigger Than a Cement Truck

It was misty on that morning
    As I set out for my jog;
Then I saw a cement truck
    Coming through the fog.
Now I consider myself fit,
    Brave, and even strong,
But up against that cement truck
    I wouldn't last for long.
So I stood well aside
    And let it have its way;
Funny how that truck
    Didn't wait for my okay.
It seems to make a lot of sense
    Not to fight with things much bigger,

And I think that's how most of us
    See the world today, I figure.
So it occurs to me
    That it's stupid, not just odd,
To make way for a cement truck
    And try to put the brakes on God.

Chapter Nine

The Seagull Looked

The Seagull Looked

Wings outstretched and ready,
    It dances on the breeze,
The seagull's flight a miracle
    Achieved with greatest ease.
It watches me intently
    As it floats on ocean sky,
For it desires the cracker
    That my fingers hold up high.
It looks into my eyes,
    Still somewhat suspicious.
Is it worth the risk?
    For the cracker looks—delicious!
Suddenly it dives!
    Plucks the cracker from my hand,
And I hear its happy cries
    As it soars above the sand.
Two minds somehow connected
    When the seagull looked at me,
And it knew the gift I held
    Was offered it for free.
And I wonder if the face God sees
    Shows much the same surprise
When I brave to take His precious gift
    And see the love that's in His eyes.

Don't Scratch!

I tried to take the cat
　　To the door the other day,
But she scratched me pretty good
　　When she tried to get away.
She likes to look outside;
　　She wants to fly just like a bird.
But to really go there?
　　That's worse than just absurd!
She knows I wouldn't hurt her,
　　But she panics just the same—
Like people who get frightened
　　And look for God to blame.
I guess it's only natural
　　To be afraid when we don't know,
But wouldn't God protect us
　　If He asked for us to go?
Perhaps I should reflect a bit
　　And not scratch like my old cat,
Decide the Lord knows best for once—
　　He'd be surprised at that!

Ivan the Terrier

A little bark, a tiny dog,
　　No bigger than a minute,
But play a game of tug-of-war
　　And that dog thinks that he'll win it!
I lift the rope and there he hangs,
　　Rope clenched between his jaws;
He spins and wriggles in the air
　　Madly waving all four paws.
I set him down to see
　　If he'll finally give it up,
But he thinks he's winning now—
　　I'll have to show that pup!

I take the rope away,
>Say, "NO! That's it!"
But though I think it's over
>Ivan simply will not quit.
It's always the persistent one
>Who wins our backyard game,
And if you don't give up your dreams
>You'll find that life is just the same.
He's the smallest dog in any hunt
>But his spirit knows no barrier.
Want to win against all odds?
>Watch Ivan, the tenacious terrier!

Amall the Llama

Some say that he was born that way,
>Feet first and looking back;
He walked backward all the time
>Often stumbling far off track.
They dragged him by a rope
>To make him walk correctly,
But on the trail he turned around
>And they shook their heads abjectly.
He never saw the trees he bumped
>Or the craters that he stepped in;
Amall didn't know where he was going,
>Only where he'd been.
One day he took a mountain trail
>That took a sharp corner to the right;
Amall kept going straight,
>Off a cliff and out of sight!
It's good to learn from your mistakes
>(That's reasoned rationale),
But keep your eyes on where you're headed
>Or end up like Amall.

Opaki...I Mean, Okapi!

I saw an opaki at the zoo;
    It almost made me laugh!
Its bottom's like a zebra's
    And its neck's from a giraffe.
In between it's like a horse
    And always wearing khaki,
But that's the way God made them
    So I'd hardly call it tacky.

When God made the first opaki
    What did He have in mind?
Did He make the opaki first
    And a zebra from its behind?
This kind of speculation
    Seems to me to be quite wacky,
For God makes us all uniquely—
    Both people and opaki.

I could not find opaki
    In any literature,
For I had misspelled the name
    Of this creature so obscure.
But a rose by another name
    Still makes your nostril's happy,
And God makes us all uniquely—
    Both people and okapi.

My mother's from New England,
    My father hails from Texas,
So to stress the "O" or "Kapi"
    Really does perplex us.
But with dachshund or dalmatian,
    A baby dog is still a puppy,
And God creates us all uniquely—
    Both people and okapi.

The possibilities are endless,
    Too much for my small brain,
So I asked my English teacher
    Which syllable to strain.
She didn't hesitate at all,
    And quickly spoke up "P."
And God creates us each uniquely—
    Both people and Okapi.

The Llama's Bunny Ears

I'm going to tell a story
    That I have found quite funny
About a llama who ate carrots
    And grew ears just like a bunny.
It carried baskets in its mouth
    Full of Easter eggs,
But it could not do the hopping
    For it had no bunny legs.
And even if it had them
    Such little legs would never do,
So it went "Down Under"
    To become a kangaroo!
And even though its legs grew strong
    And it could do a nimble crouch,
The llama was just way too big
    To fit into that pouch.
It would never be a kangaroo
    Or a bunny that could hop;
This bit of being someone else
    Would simply have to stop.
The llama decided to become
    The best llama it could be,
And when I want to do things well
    I'll start by being me.

The llama has been quite happy
    To this very day,
But a happy llama spits a lot
    So you'd best stand well away!

The Eagle's View

Level with the eagle's eye
    I find a grander view,
For from this lofty perch I see
    His promises are true.
Long I've watched the eagle
    As I stood so far below,
But now I've climbed the mountain
    And what I thought before, I know.
For I can see the valley
    And mountain silhouette;
The journey and the lesson
    Are ones I won't forget.
Now even with the eagle
    I feel my spirit soar.
Can it somehow be
    That God gives even more?
How far? How high? How free
    In this earthly body frail?
Above the eagle's eye I rise
    On life's eternal trail!

Chapter Ten

I Don't Wanna Kiss a Llama

I Don't Wanna Kiss a Llama

I don't wanna kiss a llama,
      Though they're cute I must admit,
But when they pucker up
      It's 'cause they're gonna spit!
I don't wanna kiss a giraffe,
      They stand much too tall you see;
I'd have to stand on tiptoes
      Just to kiss one on the knee.
I'd never kiss an elephant,
      Its skin is much too tough;
Besides, its trunk gets in the way
      And my lips aren't long enough!
I wouldn't kiss a penguin
      On its orange-colored beak;
I'm afraid it might take out an eye
      When it pecked me on the cheek!
But I would kiss a llama,
      Penguin, or giraffe;
I'd even kiss an elephant
      If it would make you laugh.
Yes, I would give a kiss
      To each animal at the zoo,
But I'd rather save them all
      And give every one to you!

King Louie's Horse's Butt: A Love Story

An art museum for the fair,
    St. Louie in ought-four,
And a statute of his highness
    Like he's riding out the door.
The museum's full of treasures
    From the Louvre and old King Tut,
But as I leave I come face to face
    With King Louie's horse's butt!

It doesn't seem appropriate
    At his big tail to stare,
And I wonder what they did
    To get it so high up in the air.
A girl came up behind me,
    She smiled so I said, "What?"
She said, "I think that yours is cuter
    Than King Louie's horse's butt."

I was quite astounded
    But I kind of liked the line,
And when I got to know her
    I vowed to make her mine.
We two think so much alike
    As from one stone we're cut,
So the two of us got married
    Under King Louie's horse's butt!

We still visit the museum
    And walk in Forest Park,
And at night we hold each other's hands
    And kiss there in the dark.
If I tell you where we like to kiss
    You'll think that I'm a nut:
We stand in moonlit shadows
    Of King Louie's horse's butt!

I know the statute will be there
     When we are old and grey,
For our love, like that old horse's butt,
     Will never go away.
And on our anniversary
     Up museum steps I'll strut
To kiss my wife and wave
     At King Louie's horse's butt!

I wonder what we look like
     From that pedestal above
And where our tale would rank
     In the history of love.
But you would be quite lucky
     Before life's book is shut
If you could have a love like ours
     And King Louie's horse's butt.

The Two-Toed Sloth Learns to Count

One was easy, so was two;
     Each toe he had gave him a clue.
A paw was free, then he counted to three;
     With five toes and a tail he clung to the tree.
His head hung down when he counted to four,
     But with toed back feet he could do more.
On one of them he counted five and six;
     He impressed his friends with mathematical tricks.
In the back of his mind a voice said, "Wait!"
     But he bravely went on to seven and eight.
Survival instincts did not yet fail;
     From the highest limb he still hung by his tail.
If he'd have stopped there he would have been fine,
     But the two-toed sloth counted to nine.

Super-Frog Gets a Gig

Famous for his feats of strength,
    He had much more than brawn:
Super-Frog had a mighty voice
    That just went on and on.
He cried out in the night
    Over hill and dale,
And they traveled many miles
    Just to hear that big frog wail.
He got a gig outside of Vegas,
    Just a few blocks from "The Strip";
With a voice just like Sinatra
    How that frog could lip!
But soon the novelty wore off,
    The crowds grew smaller and fewer,
And the critics used more than words
    To put Super-Frog on a skewer!
They gave a farewell banquet
    And how that big frog croaked.
Super-Frog was really hot that night;
    He cooked so much, he smoked!
Super-Frog, oh Super-Frog,
    Why did you take that gig?
Yes, they roast celebrities,
    But you're the first one on a twig!

Friday the Thirteenth

I am not superstitious
    So I do not fear this day,
But the IRS sent me a bill
    That I forgot to pay.
This morning as I jogged
    A dog chased me down the street;

On the drive into work
    The rain turned into sleet.
The bank sent me a letter;
    They turned down my credit.
That might get me down
    But today I will not let it.
The kids are sick, the dog threw up,
    My wife has got a cold.
Her birthday present I put on reserve
    Was accidentally sold.
I see no smiles of greeting;
    Every face is grim.
At work today they snarl at me
    And I snarl back at them.
But I insist that all is well
    And everything's just fine,
For it might be a bad day in your life
    But it's a normal one in mine!

Oh Christmas Treed

Our kitten's name is Star;
    She loves our Christmas tree.
On Christmas Eve she climbed it,
    For the top was the place to be.
We were all asleep
    So the house was very quiet;
The tree was lit for Santa
    And Star made up her mind to try it.
It was difficult to climb the tree,
    Past branches, ornaments, wires,
But whenever there's a mystery
    A cat always inquires.
She got stuck just below the star
    And knocked it crooked with her paw,

So when Santa came down the chimney
    The crooked star is what he saw.
Now Santa is a nice old chap
    And the star must be just right,
But when Santa reached into the tree
    He left his boots in fright!
Star hissed and scratched and clawed
    And Santa,—Quick!—drew back his hand!
But his sleeve was stuck in tinsel
    And he pulled the tree out from its stand.
The tree, the cat, and Santa
    All landed on the rug,
Then Santa saw the frightened cat,
    Smiled, and gave a shrug.
"Who booby-trapped this star
    With a little kitty cat?
It's been fifty years at least
    Since I've been scared like that!"
He got the cat untangled
    And she drank milk from Santa's cup;
He ate all the Christmas cookies,
    Then put the tree back up.
He filled the room with presents,
    Emptying his sack,
In thanks, I think, that he survived
    This terrible attack.
He went on up the chimney
    And rode off in his sleigh.
"Merry Christmas to all," he called,
    "And lock that cat away!"

Santa's New Suit

Torn and ragged, covered in soot,
    It took a century,

But Santa's suit was beyond the means
    Of elven stitchery.
They checked it out at Macy's,
    But such suits do not come cheap;
So Santa sent the brownies
    To look for ten red sheep.
They searched from Arctic plains
    To isles of the Bahamas.
Not a crimson sheep was found
    But they did find ten red llamas.
Santa rolled his eyes way back
    And shook his doleful head,
"I get a rash from llama hair,
    It makes my skin all red!"
But Christmas Eve was coming soon
    And Santa's suit was stitched,
But even with a liner
    The llama hair still itched.
Yes, it is a shame his suit was made
    With scratchy llama hair,
But it makes Santa's cheeks all rosy red,
    Both top and bottom pair.

            Inspired by a comment by Mary Kay Bertholf

An Apology to Camels

It has been pointed out to me
    That I've maligned the camel;
To be sure it's not intentional,
    For it's such a noble mammal.
Camels are much like people,
    Now that I think of it,
'Cause just like baseball players
    They chew a lot and spit!
Then there's that hump upon the back
    Nearly the size of a large boulder;

People carry chips that size
    But always on the shoulder.
A lady camel has long lashes
    Like my gal, so prim and proper,
And when either one makes up her mind
    There's just no way to stop her.
They say that camel odor's bad
    But I cannot really tell,
'Cause people like to stir things up
    And make things really smell!
Yes, I see that I have erred,
    Been badly in the wrong,
But to make it up to them
    I'll sing the camel song:

I went riding on a camel
    Into the desert sands;
The camel took me safely
    Through these barren lands.
A fortnight without water—
    I know, I did the math—
And my camel smells just fine
    'Cause I haven't had a bath!

My camel is a friendly sort
    To carry me around;
It's succeeded just three times
    To throw me to the ground!
But it really is the social type,
    It shares its friends with me.
There's only one big problem:
    Its best friend is a flea!

I am proud of my nice camel,
    It is my one true friend;
It helped me write this song
    And gave it a good end.

For I had gone to thank it,
    Bent over for some grass,
Then that nasty camel
    Bit me on the...DON'T ASK!

BUT—now I can't sit down!
    No, you may not have a look!
Don't let your mother read this song
    Or she'll throw away my book!

Our llamas are not camels. Thank God!

Epilogue

As a writer I sometimes seek solitude and quiet but am inspired by the actions of the people and animals around me. I'm always looking for that special connection to write about and to share. And it's the sharing that makes the time alone worth taking. Perhaps this poem will give some insight. God bless you.

A Lone Connection

The birds all flock together
    At the top of that tall tree
Except one that lingers here
    And stops to look at me.
I hesitate to scare it,
    For I feel a strange connection.
I too sit alone,
    Do I also need correction?
For the flock is calling out
    And warning it of danger;
A man who sits and writes alone
    Is certainly a stranger.
I slowly change my gaze
    And we're seeing eye to eye;
Then I close to let it go,
    But I can feel it fly.
It's good to be alone sometimes,
    Best together when you roam,
And so I put my things away
    And I, too, head for home.

With the continued blessing of the Holy Spirit, my next book will be *Diamonds of the Dawn*. I hope that one or more of my poems will make a connection with you! Thanks for reading.

Yours in Christ,

Byron von Rosenberg
House Springs, MO
October 12, 2003

Order Form

❑ YES, I want _____ copies of *Climb the Red Mountain* at $ 11.95 each.

❑ YES, I want _____ copies of *Don't Feed the Seagulls* at $ 11.95 each.

❑ YES, I am interested in having Byron von Rosenberg speak to my company, association, school, or organization. Please send information.

❑ YES, please inform me when *Diamonds of the Dawn* and subsequent books are published.

Postal orders: Red Mountain Creations
P.O. Box 172
High Ridge, MO 63049

Telephone orders: 1-866-SEAGULS (1-866-732-4857)

E-mail orders: redmountain@swbell.net

Website: www.byronvonrosenberg.com

Please send these books and information to:

Name: _____

Organization: _____

Address: _____

City: _____ State: _____ Zip: _____

Telephone: (_____) _____

E-mail: _____

My check or money order for $_____ is enclosed. Include shipping and state taxes.

Please charge my: Visa / MasterCard (circle one)

Card #: _____ Exp. date: _____

Book Price: $11.95 each

Shipping: $3.00 for the first book and $1.00 for each additional book to cover shipping and handling within US, Canada, and Mexico. International orders add $6.00 for the first book and $2.00 for each additional book.

Or order from:
**ACW Press • 85334 Lorane Hwy • Eugene, OR 97405
(800) 931-BOOK**

Or contact your local bookstore

Don't Feed the Seagulls

"Daddy, you can't feed the seagulls here," said my son,
  "It say's so on that sign.
If you do you'll have to pay
  'Cause there's a hundred-dollar fine."
But the seagulls must not have read those words
  And hungry they must be
For them to take a cracker
  From a lawbreaker like me.
As I hold each cracker high
  The seagulls gather to be fed,
Like famished spirits waiting
  For what nourishes much more than bread.
"Do not feed the seagulls!"
  In China or Bangladesh,
For we're afraid what will happen here
  If they taste what's good and fresh.
But yes, I WILL feed the seagulls
  On this or any beach,
And I will spread the gospel
  Until the whole wide world I reach.

from *Don't Feed the Seagulls*